Collectible

Girlie Glasses

Tigre McMullan

Schiffer Publishing Ltd

4880 Lower Valley Road, Atglen, PA 19310 USA

Acknowledgments

There are many people I wish to thank for their assistance and inspiration for this project: Olga, my wife, who has the heart of a saint and the patience to match, especially when we come to another flea market or estate sale; Anne Bartok and Rudy Le CoaDic for their persistence and joy in seeing me begin, work on, and complete the book; Adam Chinitz for his expertise and humor, and Xavier Brunet for the loan of equipment. I would also thank Patrick Pigott, Ann Borthwick, Tom Becker, and the many others who lent their support and expertise to the book.

Contents

Library of Congress Card Number: 2003101050

Cover and book design by: Bruce Waters
Type set in Zurich Bik heading font/text font Zurich BT

ISBN: 0-7643-1862-4
Printed in China
1 2 3 4

Published by Schiffer Publishing Ltd.
4880 Lower Valley Road
Atglen, PA 19310
Phone: (610) 593-1777; Fax: (610) 593-2002
E-mail: Info@schifferbooks.com
Please visit our web site catalog at
www.schifferbooks.com
We are always looking for people to write books on new and related subjects. If you have an idea for a book please contact us at the above address.

This book may be purchased from the publisher.
Include $3.95 for shipping.
Please try your bookstore first.
You may write for a free catalog.

In Europe, Schiffer books are distributed by
Bushwood Books
6 Marksbury Ave.
Kew Gardens
Surrey TW9 4JF England
Phone: 44 (0) 20 8392-8585; Fax: 44 (0) 20 8392-9876
E-mail: Bushwd@aol.com
Free postage in the U.K., Europe; air mail at cost.

Dedication

When I thought about dedicating this book to someone, I had a hard time trying to decide who it should be. There are so many people who deserve the thanks and credit for so much. So I decided to dedicate it to two people: my grandfather, Richard D. McMullan, the first collector I came to know and recognize; and my father, Richard K. McMullan, who always inspires me.

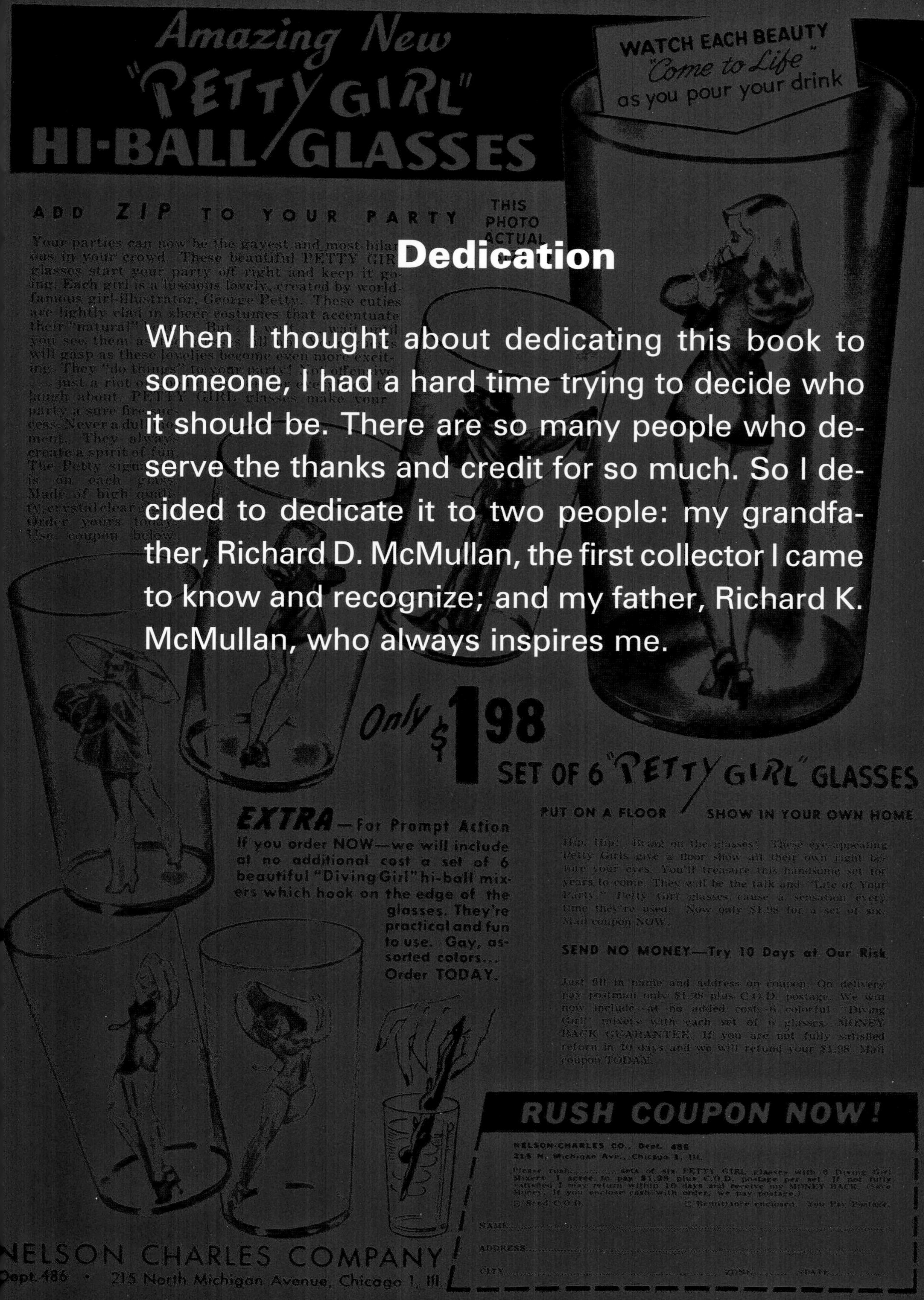

Foreword

Like many collectors, I have been asked how I began my collection. The story starts in Connecticut. Olga and I were driving from Boston to New York and were getting tired of I-95. So we decided to pull off the interstate and drive on the side routes through some of the towns that we had heard were good for antiquing. We spent many hours on many roads, in many towns, stopping at many stores, but finding that we were in an area that specialized in antiques that were not in our price range or tastes. They were beautiful, but we could not afford them and could not see ourselves living with them. It was around five in the evening and stores were closing, when we decided to head back to the interstate to get home. We were driving on a side road that was supposed to bring us back to I-95 when we passed a small sign that said "antiques." I turned to Olga and asked if it was a store. She said she guessed so. When I asked if she wanted to stop at it, she thought about it and then said, "If you think it's open, why not?"

Pulling into the drive, we were not sure what we had found. It looked like someone's home, but the garage doors were open, and after a moment of hesitation, we went in to explore. Everything was in boxes, dusty, stacked, without tags, labels, or prices. We were about to leave, thinking this could not be a real shop, when an older woman came out to us and told us that this was her garage. The store was on the back porch, but we were free to look through her garage if we wanted to, and anything we wanted, we should just bring it into the house and she would sell it to us. We decided to go into the house to look at the real store.

As we turned to leave, I saw a box between the garage doors containing three glasses with girls on them. The girls had white dresses. One was a bride, another was holding an umbrella. They looked cool, so I brought them with me. Moving inside, we were amazed. The entire first floor of the house was filled with glassware, pottery, and silverware. You name it and you could find some there. We spent what felt like hours exploring new rooms full of the stuff we just loved: Depressionware, salt and pepper shakers, and a set of three glasses each with a hand-painted cockfight scene were just some of the items. When we had decided we had gathered as much as we could find, we went to pay for the stuff. The woman saw the girlie glasses and told me her daughter had just found them. She thought the clothes might disappear when you put cold water inside. The woman didn't really know, she hadn't tested them. She noticed that we liked Depressionware and asked if we had looked inside the cabinets behind us. There was so much stuff on top and in front, we hadn't thought to look inside. So back we went, finding more stuff. It took a few trips, for us to finally walk out of the store. That is how I got my first three glasses.

When people ask me where the store is, I can't tell them. I don't know. I don't remember what town we were in. I don't remember which road. I wish I did. Now it is years later, and those three glasses, which seemed like a small find amidst a whirlwind, have turned into their own storm. I hope you enjoy this part of my collection as much as I do. Collecting them has been a blast, and I love to show them off. I still just think they are cool.

Introduction

In their heyday of the 1940s and 1950s, you could find pinup girls on calendars, pens, cigarette lighters, ads, light fixtures, books, and other household items. One of the most popular items of the time was the pinup glass. On the glass, there is a decal of a lady. On one side she is fully clothed, but when the glass is turned around or liquid poured in, the glass reveals a risqué look at the same woman. These glasses were sold in catalogs like Johnson and Smith and magazines like Esquire. Families sent the glasses to soldiers oversees to cheer them up. They were given away as carnival prizes, sold as souvenirs, and raffled off in the neighborhood stores. Victory Glass sets were bought to show support for the armed forces during World War II. A second set of the glasses was made to show support for the homefront volunteers. The Amus-U Company created a line of glasses that magically made the girls clothing disappear when cold liquid was poured into the glass. The Meyercord Decal and Duro Decal Companies not only sold sets of the glasses, but also the decals, which you could then place on anything you wanted. Other companies put out keyhole glasses, where you look through a keyhole on the back of the glass to see the revealing picture. The art of two of the most well known pinup artists, Vargas and Petty, was put on glasses and decal sets. Many other popular artists' styles were copied for use on them. Americans, it seemed, could not get enough of these glasses.

This book is a catalogue of some of the sets I have found. The more I have researched them, the more I discover. Enjoy.

Chapter One

Meyercord and the Nudie Cuties

Based in Chicago, Meyercord® was one of the major decal companies from the 1930s to the 1950s. Many credit Meyercord with being the first company to make pinup decals available. They created decal sets under the title of "Nudie Cuties" that you could put on anything you desire. I have seen them on pitchers, trays, briefcases, in the movie The Manchurian Candidate, and even on a couple of cars.

A decal set in original packaging goes for about $30. A full set of the glasses is around $150, or $25 apiece. This set includes one bride, two bridesmaids, a socialite, a milkmaid, and a gypsy dancer.

Also from Meyercord, this second set of "Nudie Cuties" has three gypsy dancers, an Indian dancer, a flower girl, and a hula dancer. Value is similar to the first set at $150 for the set or $25 per glass.

Chapter Two

Duro-Decal and Jaco-Lac

Another major company based in Chicago in the 1940s was Duro-Decal®. Although it was a smaller company, they seem to have put out many more of the girlie-style decals. The earliest did not have the greatest detail, but later decals improved in design and added a dash of humor.

This is the Duro-Decal Beach Set with a total of eight decals, simple in design, and limited in detail. They do, however, have nice coloration. $30 for the full sheet of the decals. A full set of glasses is hard to find, but partial sets are common. $180 for a full set, $22 for a single glass.

An advertisement from the Johnson & Smith Company® catalog for this set of glasses. You could also get the decal set separately. Also on this page, you can see the Mystic glass set for sale at a very reasonable price.

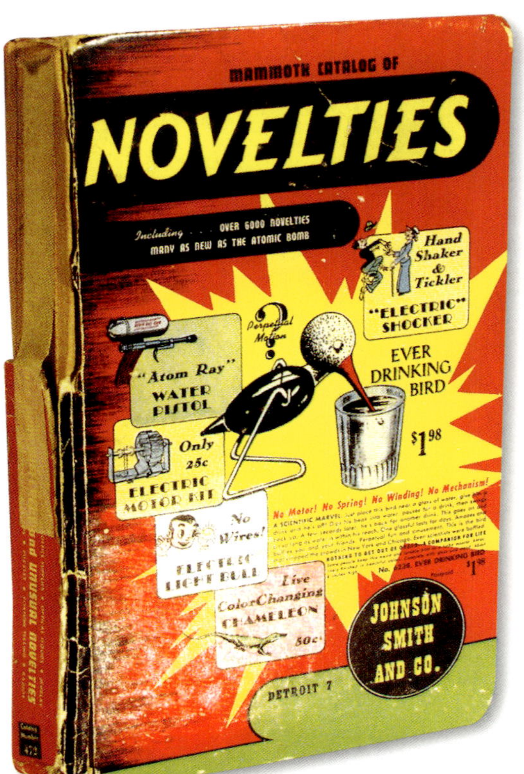

Duro-Decal sheet 1128. This set has better detail in the decals. Sheet of Decals $30. A full set of glasses costs $150, and a single glass is $25.

Duro-Decal sheet 1129. This set also has plenty of detail in the decals. Sheet of Decals $50. A full set of glasses costs $200 and a single glass is $25.

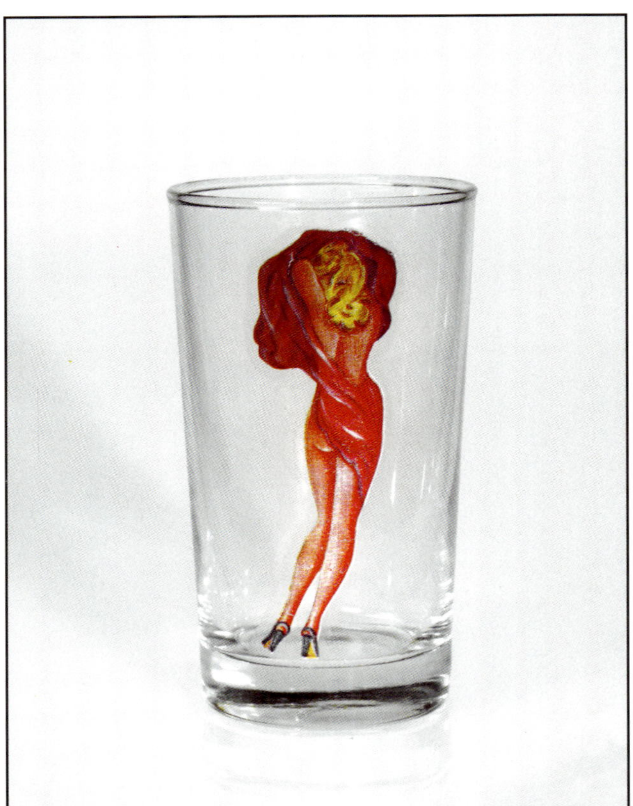

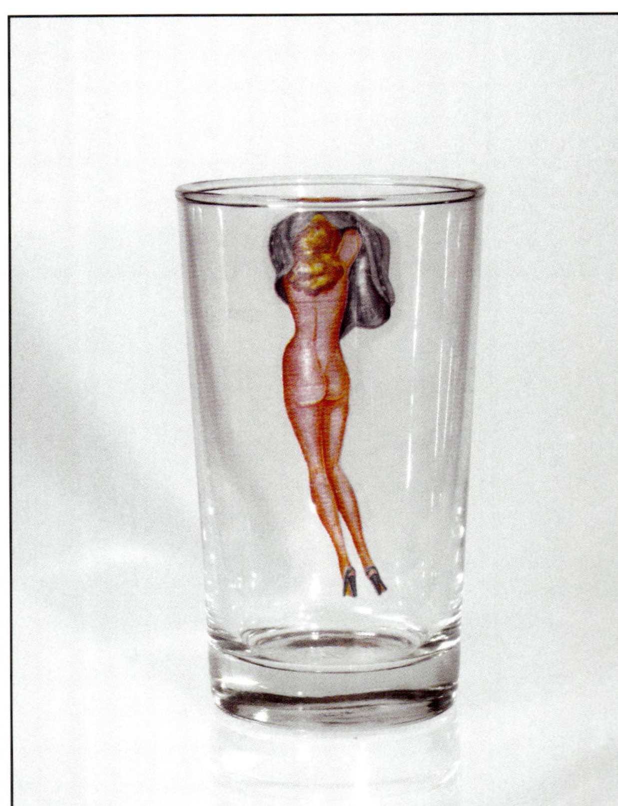

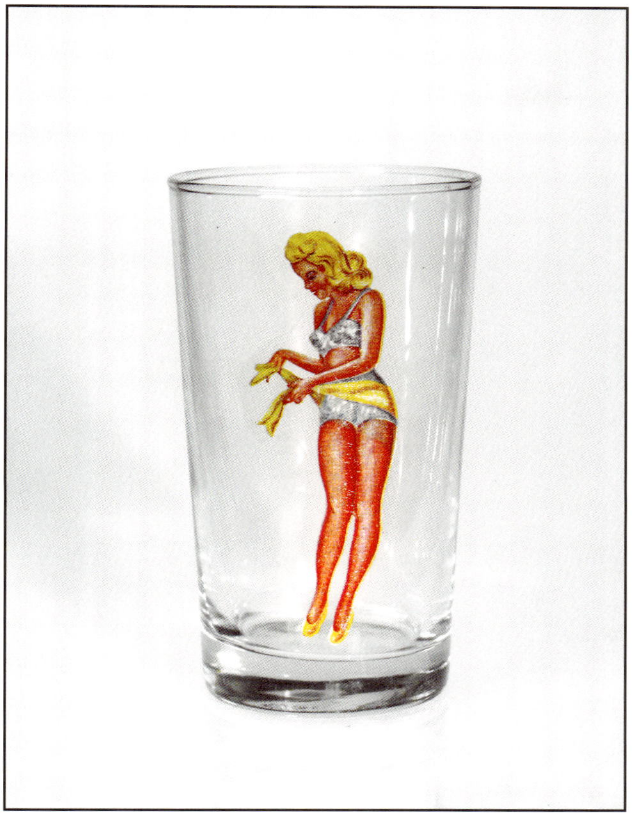

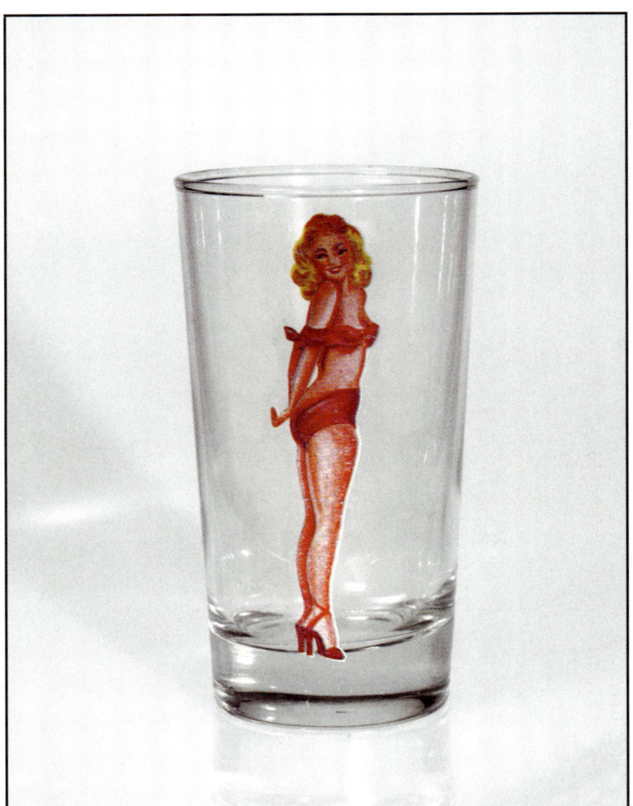

Duro-Decal sheet 270. A later set with a wonderful sense of humor. $50 for the sheet. A full set of the glasses costs around $180, or $30 for a single glass.

This woman is hitchhiking with a leg exposed. Reminiscent of the movie "It Happened One Night," it was risqué in its time simply for that reason. The reverse side, however, shows a devil picking her up. So who is worse?

WET
PAINT

WET
PAINT

Duro-Decal sheet 271. A later set with a wonderful sense of humor. $50 for the sheet. A full set of the glasses costs around $200, or $30 for a single glass.

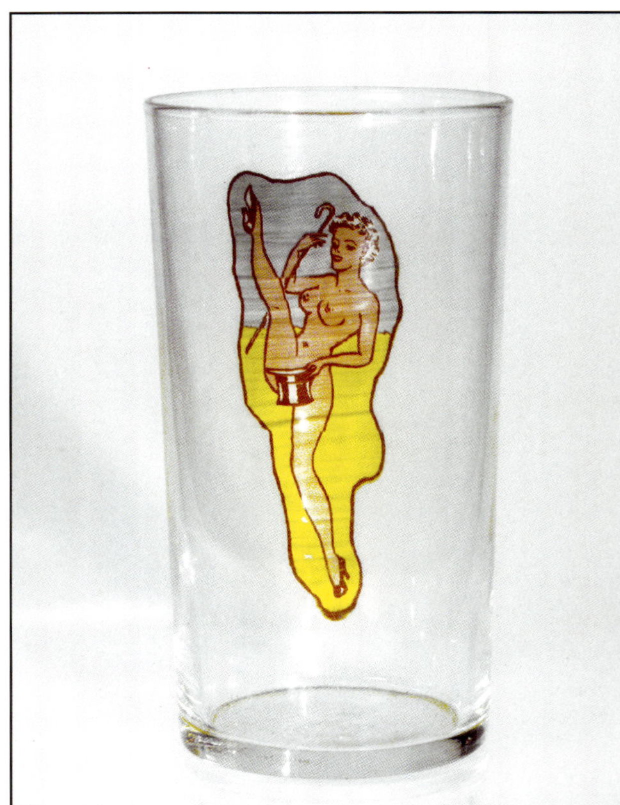

Duro-Decal sheet 272. A later set with a wonderful sense of humor. Take note of the kissing booth fantasy and the strategic hat placement in the men at work decal. $50 for the sheet. A full set of the glasses costs around $200, or $30 for a single glass.

KISSES
$1
CHARITY
BAZAAR

KISSES
$1

Duro-Decal sheet 216. A later set with a wonderful artwork. $50 for the sheet. A full set of the glasses costs around $200, or $30 for a single glass.

Jaco-Lac®, also put out decal sets in the 1940s. Their "Nudie Beauties" sets were very detailed and popular. Decal sets were originally priced at 35 cents, but now go for $30. Glasses are around $20 per glass, and full glass sets from $120 to $140.

This "Hula-Hula Girls" set is very detailed and highly collectable. $200 for the set or $35 for a single glass.

This glass includes a small torn decal at the top saying it is a souvenir of Randolf, Vermont. The decal was sold in sheets, and could be put on almost any item to make it special for the location. This additional decal doesn't add any value to the glass unless the place itself has some value to the collector.

Jaco-Lac sheet 404. Not as detailed as their "Hula-Hula Girls" set but still a very high quality set. Set value is $120, or $20 for each glass.

Chapter Three

Mystic, Magic, and the Disappearing Clothes

One of the more interesting types of glasses to come out was created by the Amus-U-Line. Called Mystic Girlie Glasses, the "mystic" action was to have a covering over the girl that would disappear when cold liquid was put into the glass.

Many of the sets you see today have lost their clothes due to washing. The cover over the decals would wash off if not cleaned gently by hand or if left to soak.

I found this advertisement for "Mystic Action Hollywood Pin-up Glasses" in *Movie Play* magazine from November 1946. A full copy of the magazine can cost around $15; just the page can be around $5.

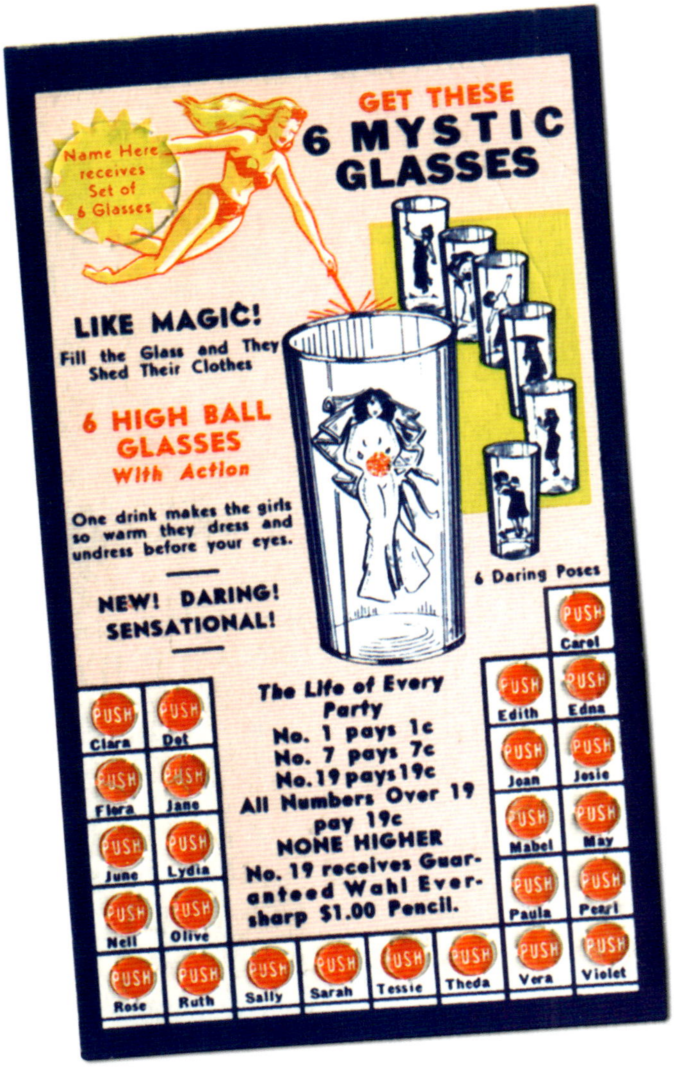

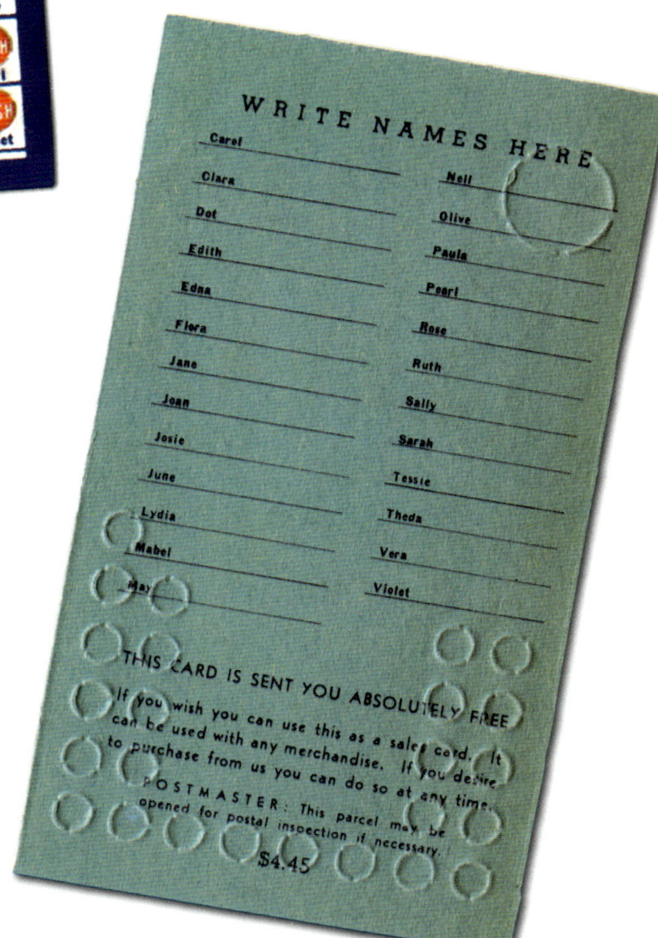

Advertisement punch card. This punch card would be sent to the retailer as a promotional item. Customers would buy a punch, and the winner would get the full set of glasses. Expect to pay $20 to $25 for a punch card of this style in mint condition.

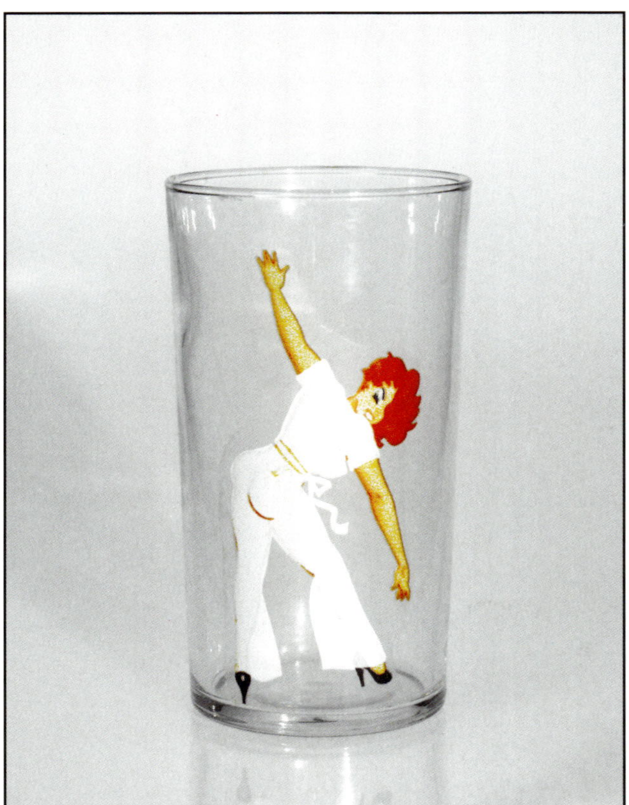

Federal Glass put out a similar set of these glasses under the name Magic Follies. Their decal showed the girls in lingerie as opposed to naked. The decals are more detailed than the Mystic glasses. $120 for a full set or $20 apiece.

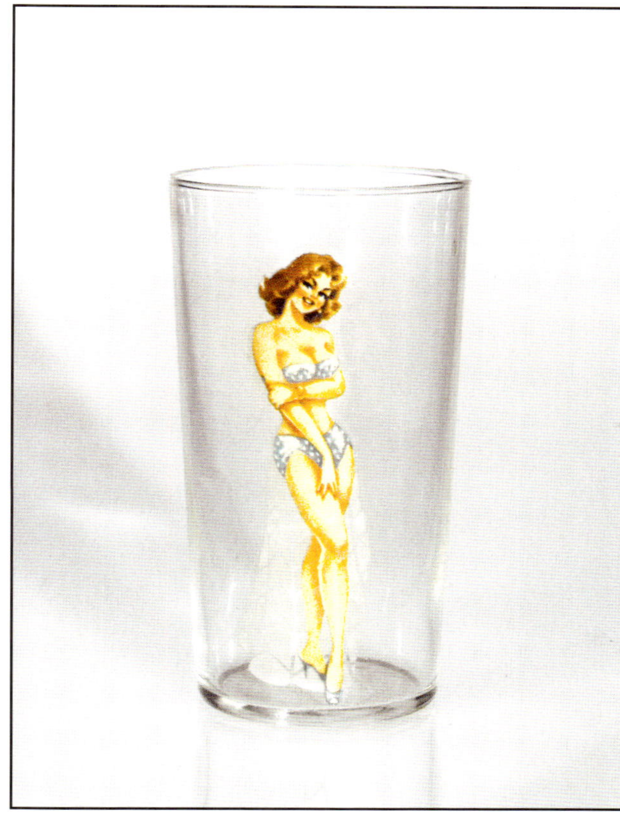

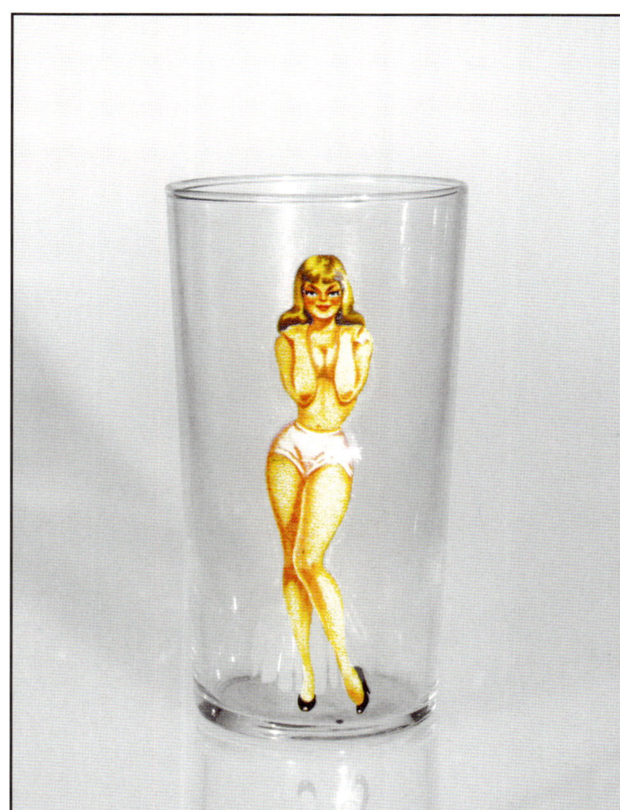

As an added incentive to order the Magic Follies Glasses, you would get the Cuties Of Ice set free with prompt payment. $20

FREE for promptness
Ice Cube Cuties
NEW ICE CUBE MOLD MAKES 4 DARING CUTIES
Here's your brand new drink sensation! Just fill mold with water, freeze and remove . . . and you've got 4 beauties in ice for your guests' drinks. Wonderful conversation maker for your next party at home, at the office, club, anywhere!
YOURS FREE...
if you send in your order within the next 15 days!

Advertising punch card for the Magic Follies set. $30

In the 1970s and 1980s, Spencer Gifts® sold the "Sip 'N Strip" glass sets; one male set and one female set, each set with 4 glasses. They took a photo decal and placed the clothes over the decals, so the condensation of the liquid in the glass would make the clothes disappear. Creating an update of the older style. $20 for a full set of the female, $30 for the male set, which is harder to find, or $5 apiece.

"Centerfold Magic Highballs" were produced by H. Fishlove and Co.® in the 1970s. They created multiple sets of females, couples, and male and female African-Americans.

Two Glasses from the African-American Male set. $60 for the set, or $15 for a glass.

Two of the couples set. $50 for the set, or $12 for a single glass.

Another set of glasses from the same time period. Photos with an overlay of swimsuits. There are no markings on the glass to tell who created them, but they have a similar feel to the "Celebrity Glass" sets. $10 per glass.

The label reads "Made in Italy for Samag Monoco." The set includes six glasses where the shots are very fantasy oriented. The clothing disappears and leaves very little to the imagination. $90 for a full set, or $15 for a single glass.

Chapter Four

Keyhole Glasses

Keyhole glasses are a variation on the pinup glass. Some of the following sets can be found without the frosted glass and keyhole theme. Unlike other sets in this book, companies could not sell these glasses as decals. The production process was too difficult to reproduce at home.

This glass is the hardest to find of the set. Ironically, I found three of this same glass at an auction. Expect to pay $30 for the glass.

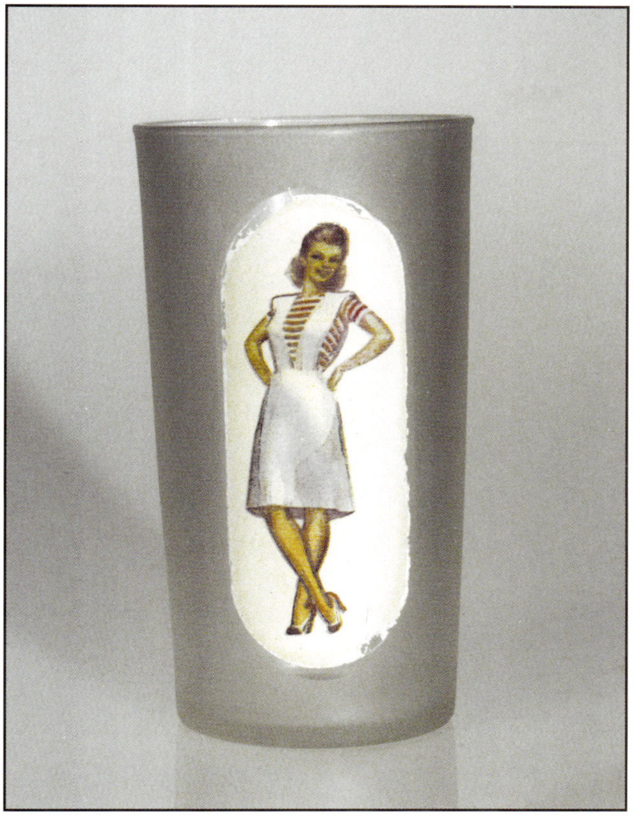

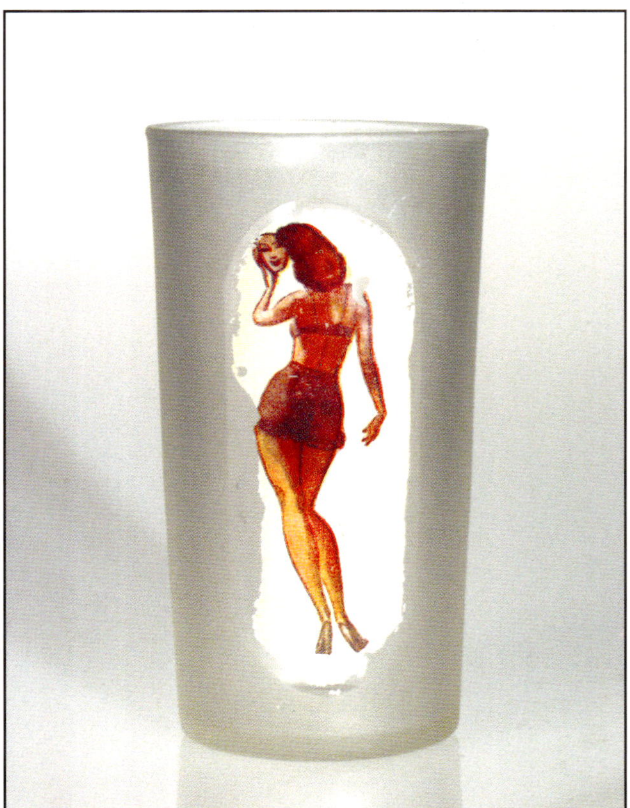

This set of five glasses is also from the 1960s. This is a common set. You can expect to pay $15 for a glass, or $70 for a complete set.

REAL FUN MAKERS
CLEVER • UNUSUAL
WATCH THE SHOW GIRLS THROUGH THE KEYHOLE!
PULL DOWN
This is what happens when you look through the keyhole of all your Show Girl Glasses. Get a full set—with all these gorgeous girls.
These dazzling Show Girls will entertain you.

REAL FUN MAKERS
CLEVER • UNUSUAL
WATCH THE SHOW GIRLS THROUGH THE KEYHOLE!
BRING KEY CLUB FUN TO YOUR NEXT PARTY
No. 1 pays 1c—No. 10 pays 10c—No. 17 pays 17c—No. 25 pays 25c. All others pay 39c. None Higher.
LUCKY NUMBERS 3, 7, 12, 14 PAY NOTHING
Lucky number under this seal wins complete set of new Show Girl Glasses.
Do Not Remove Seal Until Entire Card Is Sold

This set of eight glasses is from the 1950s. It eliminates the oval around the ladies and the keyhole is smaller. The detail on the decals is very good. A full set costs around $160. Single glasses sell for $20.

Chapter Five

International Ladies

Many of the sets that can be found have an international theme. Created around the end of World War II. These sets catered to the tastes of the returning soldiers who remembered the women they had seen overseas. Along with the glasses, art photo club magazines and card decks also carried this theme.

The following set of eight glasses features dancers, each in different dress style. There are a lot of nice detailed touches on the decals. I think the following set was made by Jaco-Lac, but I have been unable to confirm this. Cost for the set is $160, or $20 for a single glass.

This set of six glasses also features ladies with the international dancer theme. The bold colors are what make this set special. $120 for the set or $20 each.

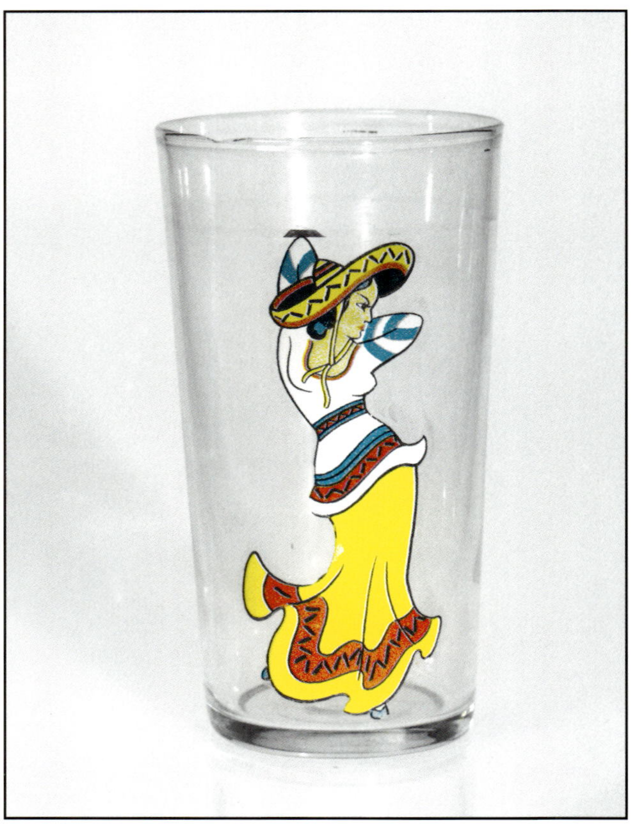

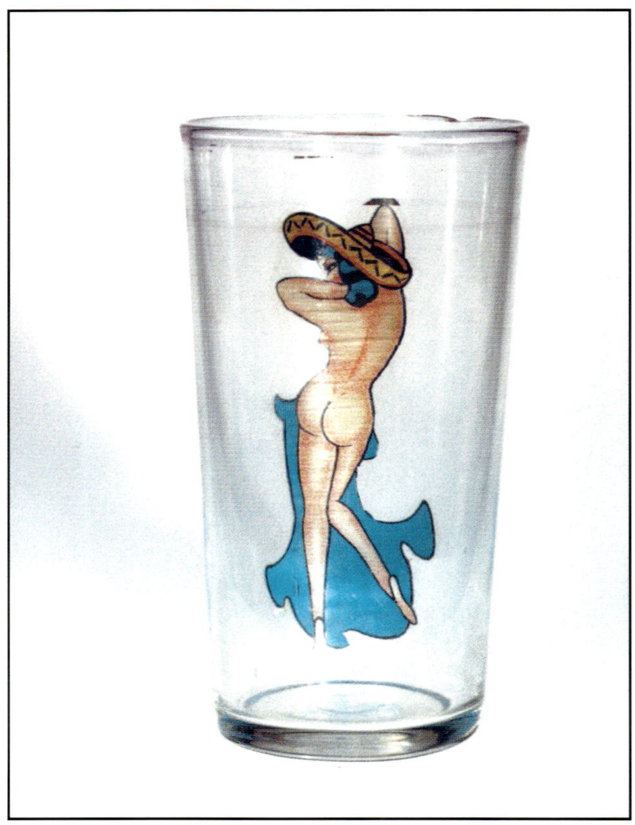

Another set of six glasses from what looks to be the same company. It has the same bold coloring and theme of the international dancers. Detail on these decals is of very high quality. A set costs $120, or $20 each glass.

Chapter Six

Shot Glasses

Since shot glasses are a separate collectible category, these glasses can be harder to come across than the larger ones. The decals on them are just as detailed as their larger counterparts, just smaller.

This set of shot glasses from the 1950s is a little worn. The decals are nicely detailed, and have an all-American, down home feel to them. $140 for a set, or $20 each.

The smallest reversible pinup decal set in my collection. These diminutive ladies are a little international, a little sporty, or just plain little. $120 for the set, or $20 each.

Chapter Seven

Signature Glasses

Some of the most famous pinup artists had sets of glasses created with their artwork. These images can also be seen on calendars, lighters, and many other items from the same period. One of the things you should look for on these glasses is the signature.

Petty is one of the premier pinup artists in the world. In the 1950s, he came out with a set of glasses based on his girls on the phone. The reveal on these glasses is an optical illusion. When liquid is put into the glass, the image becomes larger. The decals have Petty's signature on a small tail outside the main decal. When washed, this peninsula is the first part of the decal to get damaged and lost. Due to the high collectability of Petty, the cost of the set is around $240. Individual glasses can be bought for $40.

Vargas is another of the famous pinup artists. His set of six glasses has a very high quality decal with his signature near the girl's foot. Unlike the Petty glasses the signature is a more integrated part of the decal. Put out in the 1960s, this set is harder to find than the Petty set, and costs around $250. Individual glasses can be bought for $40.

Varga

Varga

Varga

Varga

Chapter Eight

Specialty Glasses

Glasses created for special occasions always have a certain quality to them. Whether for an event, location, or occasion these glasses are remembered as a treasured souvenir and a reminder of things from our past.

In 1939, San Francisco held the Golden Gate Expo. This was the same year that New York hosted the World's Fair. As a show of sisterhood, San Francisco put out this collector glass, "A Toast to the Fairs, From Coast to Coast." When the fair was over, many of the decals were left over, so someone cut the decal into two pieces and used each side on a different glass; two for the price of one. The detail on them is very good and the colors bright, but the New York girl's arm and belt are a little funky. $20 for a glass with a single girl; $60 for a full decal.

CALIFORNIA

NEW YORK

This glass is a chaperone glass from the 1940s. Made to be placed in hotel rooms, the poem is sweet: Here's to the chaperone / May she learn from Cupid / Just enough blindness / To be sweetly stupid. $25 for the glass

This German glass from the 1950s has an actual photo stuck to the glass, with a hand-painted scene on the front. The saying across the top is "The moral of the story," and the sign says "Ladies Room." $50 for the glass

Chapter Nine

Theme Glasses

Many of the sets displayed in this book have themes, but all are memorable in there own way for the artwork and detail in the decals. In the following sets, the images are strong and vibrant, and show some of the themes that were common in pinup art between the 1930s and today.

From the 1960s, the Las Vegas card girls are the first six spade cards. The decal is very detailed. $120 for the set, or $20 for each glass.

This set of glasses has remarkable decals. Looking like they're from the 1920s, the artwork and detail is fantastic. Five of the glasses have a summer sports theme, while the other three have a winter sports theme. The eyes are expressive and joyful. This is one of my favorite sets and a rare find. $240 for a set, or $30 for a single glass.

Gilchrist & King® put out this set of eight glasses in the 1980s. Made in England, each pair of glasses is a matching man and woman with the name of each character on the bottom. The decals themselves are excellent in quality and detail, and are actually two decals - one on the exterior of the glass, and one on the interior. These are $200 for a full set.

Gilchrist & King
Darling
MADE IN ENGLAND

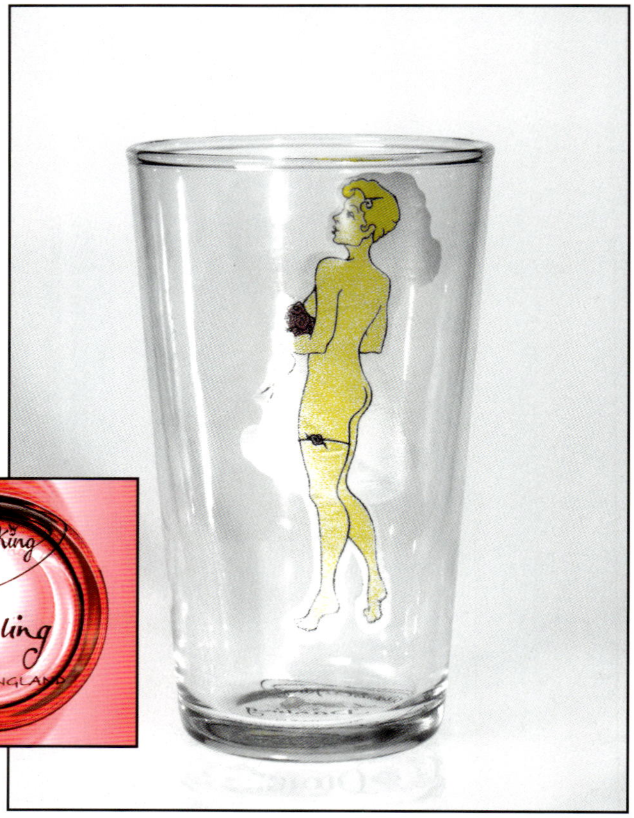

Gilchrist & King
Dearest
MADE IN ENGLAND

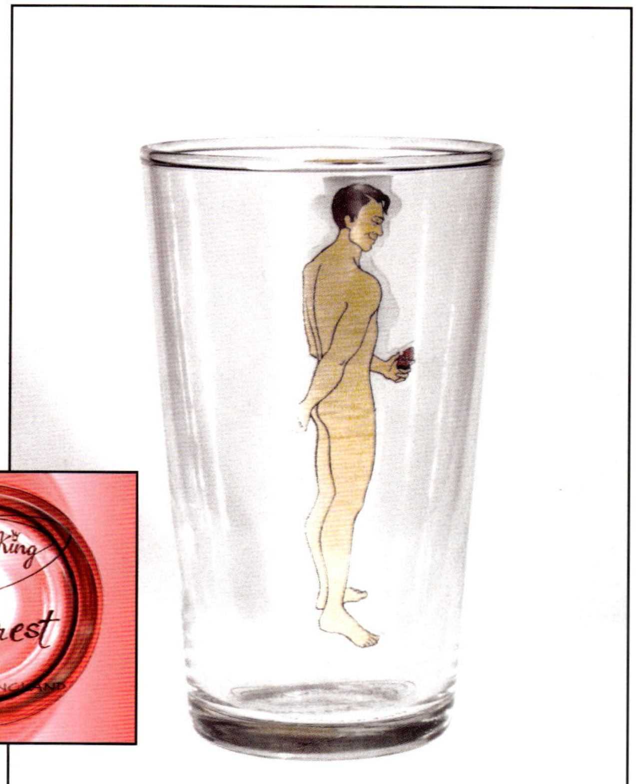

Gilchrist & King
Sunny
MADE IN ENGLAND

Gilchrist & King
Salty
MADE IN ENGLAND

Gilchrist & King
Juanita
MADE IN ENGLAND

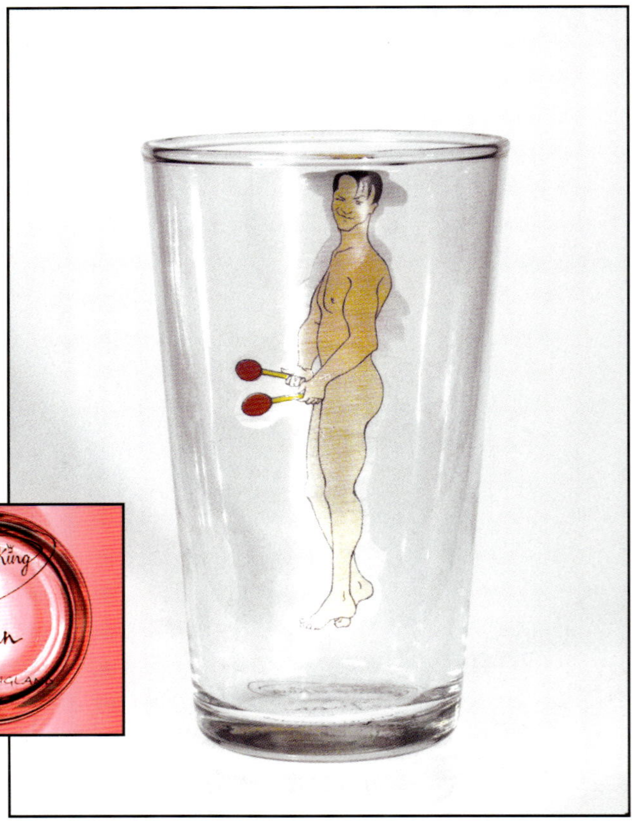

Gilchrist & King
Juan

Chapter Ten

Homefront Glasses

Sometimes called Victory glasses, these were made to show support for our armed forces during the World War II. Homefront glasses show the "V" like the Victory glass sets, but also had a theme of the returning soldier, or the defending of the shores to them. These sets are not easy to find, but are well worth the hunt.

The set that follows came in two styles. You can see the two different decals when you look at the back; one has the victory symbol in the banner above the heads of the couple, while the other does not. The reveal on this glass is very slight. You can see the girl's panties as wind blows up her skirt. This is a common motif in many of the pinups from this time. The cost of a set like this is very high, about $40 for a glass or $240 for the set. The set without the banner above the heads on the back can be as much as $300, since it is very rare.

Toast THE Navy

Salute OUR ARMY

V

KEEP 'EM ROLL'N

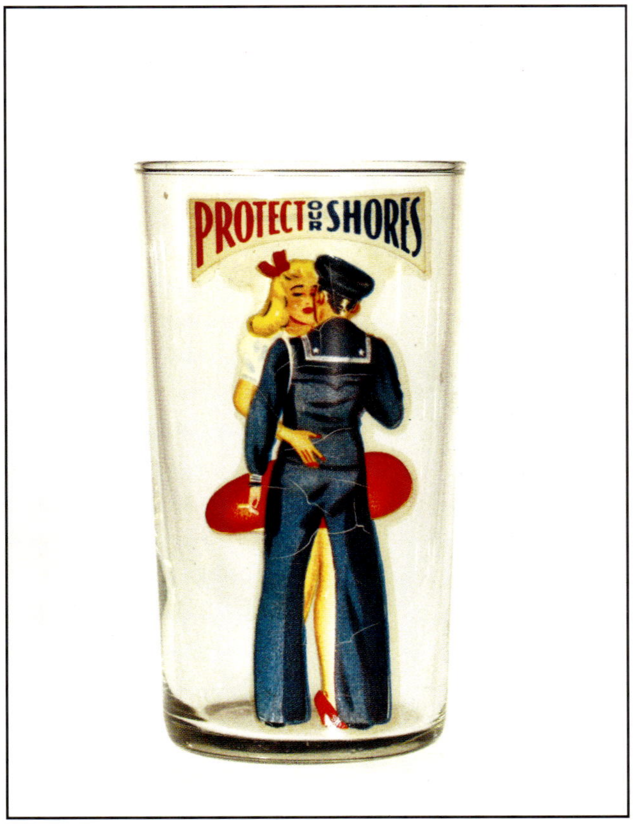
PROTECT OUR SHORES

V•••—V

When sent from the manufacturer, these sets included a free set of coasters. Now, you can expect to pay $30 for a full set.

Chapter Eleven

Hand-Painted Glasses

These designs from the 1960s are hand-painted onto the glass. Quality and detail varies greatly from glass to glass. These are not my favorite sets, but some of the individual glasses count among my favorites.

This set of seven tumblers is from the 1960s. The artist put small touches onto each of them that make them fun. The Sailor has hatch marks on her hip and the Strip Tease glass is one of my personal favorites. Expect to pay $25 per glass.

STRIP-
TEASE

This set of six pilsner glasses is from the same time period as the set of tumblers. Of interest is the African American glass. You can expect to pay $30 for a glass.

I picked up this set of five glasses in Australia. Of interest is the painting all around the glass. The lady in the stewpot with the cannibal is one of my favorites, along with the fishes smiling at the lady with the towel. Pricing on a set like this is very difficult, but expect to pay $250 to $300 for a full set.